Graeme Catna

KW-224-339

A YOUNG WORLD
TRIPPER BOOK

Created and edited by
DESMOND MARWOOD
Written by
EDWARD HOLMES
Illustrated by
PHILIP CORKE

Prepared in consultation with
FREDERICK J. WILKINSON, F.R.S.A.

in which Uncle George takes Tony and Anne on a trip to a . . .

© 1973 Thomas Nelson & Sons Limited
Printed in Great Britain by Gilmour & Dean.

castle

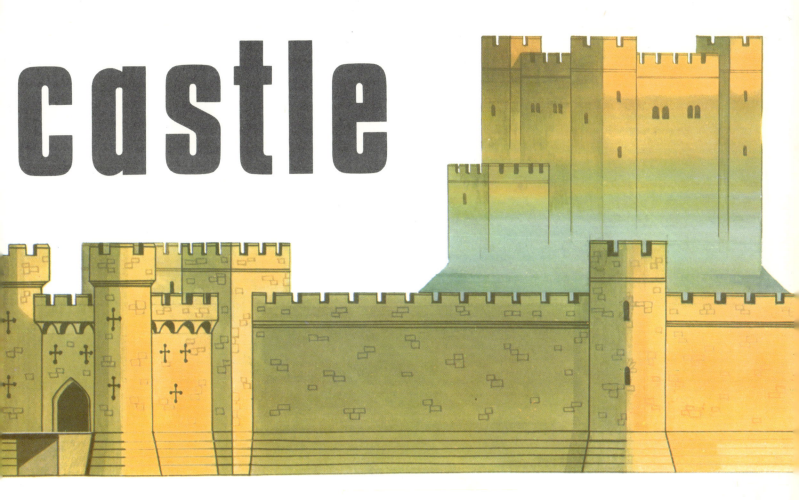

NELSON
YOUNG WORLD

A trip with Uncle George was something that Tony and his sister Anne always enjoyed. Uncle George was their favourite uncle, and he always had lots of interesting things to tell them about the places they visited.

Today they were visiting a castle. Uncle George left his car in the car park, and they finished the journey on foot. On the way, Uncle George stopped. "Now you can see how easily people on the castle walls could see you coming," he said "most castles were built in such a way that it was difficult for anyone to get near them secretly."

"A castle is really a very strong house," Uncle George explained, "the great lords and barons who lived in them in the days of long ago, built them with thick walls, and fortified them so that they and their loyal followers would be safe from enemies who attacked them. They put a high outer wall all round the outside, and then, to make it even safer, they surrounded this wall with a deep ditch, filled with water." "That's called the moat!" Said Anne. "You can only cross it by the drawbridge!"

By now they were near enough to see the bridge of heavy wooden planks that spanned the moat. "That drawbridge is the only way into the castle," Uncle George went on, "so that if the castle was attacked, they could draw it up, and there would be no way into the castle, except over the walls." "That's why it's called a drawbridge!" said Tony triumphantly. "You can draw it up!" "Right!" said Uncle George.

Across the drawbridge, on the other side of the moat, was the gate-house. Its walls towered above them, and Tony and Anne could not help thinking how easy it would be for people inside the castle to throw spears and other unpleasant things at them. They could hurl spears, or shoot arrows, through the slots in the wall-top, and then dodge behind the blocks between the slots when arrows were shot up at them.

Uncle George explained how the draw-bridge was pulled up. "In olden times," he said, "there were two big iron chains, running from the bridge and up through those slits in the wall. Inside the gate-house, in the room over the entrance tunnel, there was a machine called a windlass. Using the wind-lass, the men on duty could reel in the chains, and so hoist up the drawbridge. When it was up, it covered the entrance like a huge door."

Tony had been thinking, while Uncle George had been explaining this. "If I was a knight," he said, "I'd gallop my horse across the draw-bridge before they could pull it up. I'll bet it took quite a long time to haul this heavy bridge up by hand!" "I expect it did," agreed Uncle George, "but then they had a much quicker way of keeping you out if they wanted to." Uncle George pointed to the top of the entrance archway. "See that strong wooden lattice, with the spikes pointing downwards? That is the portcullis—and those spikes are made of iron. When they really needed to 'shut the door' in a hurry, they could just drop the portcullis—CRASH!"

It really was beginning to look as if no-body could get into a castle, unless the folks inside wanted them to!

"Notice how narrow the tunnel is," said Uncle George, "even if you got across the drawbridge, and past the portcullis, you still couldn't get a lot of men into the castle quickly."

Uncle George led the way into the entrance tunnel, and pointed upwards to where there was a round opening in the tunnel roof. "Through that hole," he said, "is the winding room, where they had the windlass for the drawbridge, and another one for the portcullis. Also, if they knew you were coming, and they didn't like you, they would boil up a cauldron of oil to pour on your head through that hole."

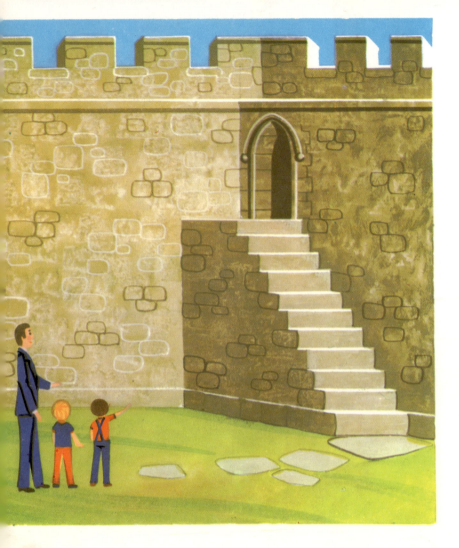

They went through the entrance tunnel, and came into a big courtyard within the castle walls. Grass had grown all over it, though here and there stone slabs were visible. "This courtyard is called the outer bailey," said Uncle George. "Apart from the visitors, it is deserted now, but once upon a time, it was a very busy place. All kinds of ordinary, everyday things went on in the outer bailey."

Uncle George pointed to some stone slabs in the ground. "Sometimes, you can pick out the foundations of a building that once stood here, or maybe these slabs were where the blacksmith stood his anvil." "Did the blacksmith make the swords and the armour for the soldiers?" Tony wanted to know. "I don't think so," replied Uncle George, "they would buy armour and weapons from the armourers in the big towns, and the very best armour came from Italy and Germany. No, the old castle blacksmith just did repairs to weapons and armour, and shod the horses."

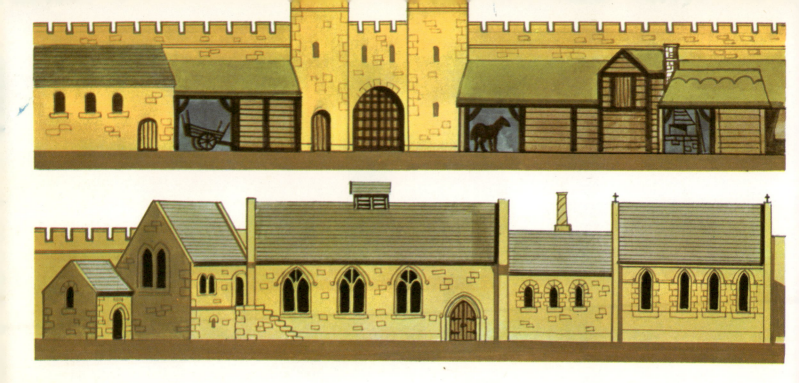

"Where did they keep all their horses?" asked Anne. "Are there stables somewhere?" "There were once." Replied Uncle George. "Usually buildings like stables and cow-byres were built of wood, inside the castle walls, and they have all rotted away and fallen down years ago."

"There were often stone buildings inside the castle walls," Uncle George went on, "but they were never built as solidly as the castle walls, and quite often they have been pulled down to use the stones for other buildings. They would have been things like chapels, and guest houses."

By this time they had walked right across the outer bailey, and on the side opposite the gate-house was a wall. It, too, had a gate-house in it, and it was defended by a moat which could be crossed by means of a second drawbridge. "This is the inner wall," said Uncle George, "it formed a second line of defence, which could be held if an enemy had got into the outer bailey."

"The enemy would have to be very strong to get through all those defences we've just seen," said Anne. "That's true," replied Uncle George, "but don't forget that enemies didn't only get in by force of arms. There were times when they got in by treachery. If some of the guards were traitors, they might be let in!"

They started to cross the drawbridge to the inner gate-house, and they could see the water-gate which connected the inner moat to the outer one.

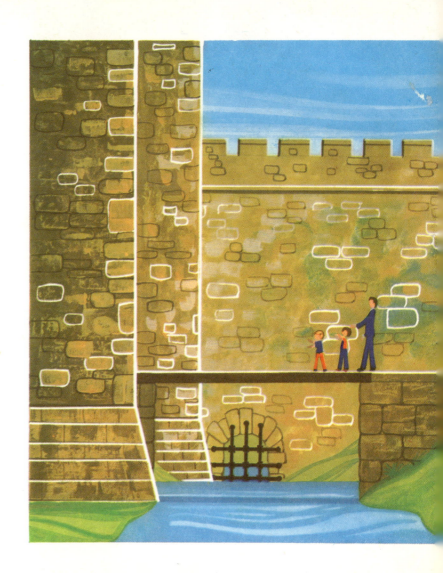

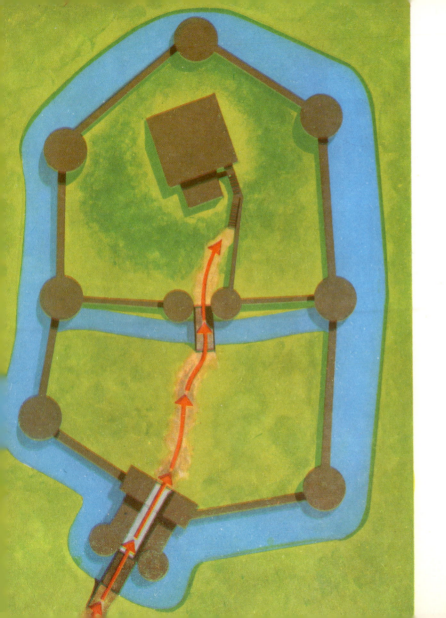

Uncle George and the children went through the inner gate-house, and there, facing them was a turreted stone building. "That's what I call a proper castle!" said Tony. "That's just what it is," Uncle George agreed. "That is the keep, the most important part of the whole castle. In the very oldest castles, the keep was the whole thing. The walls around the keep are called 'outer defences'. The keep was the last stronghold of the defenders when everything else had fallen to the enemy."

They stopped just inside the inner gate, in what Uncle George told them was called the inner bailey, while Uncle George drew a diagram for them. It showed how the various parts of the castle were arranged, and he marked in the way they had come from the front gate.

"That's better," said Anne, "now I can see how it all fits together. It's jolly hard to work out the shape of something as big as a castle, especially when you are in the middle of it!"

The ground within the inner bailey rose up in the middle, and it was on this highest part that the keep was built. "Castles are nearly always built on the top of hills, so that they command a view of the whole countryside around them. If they are attacked, then the attackers have got to fight their way up hill." Said Uncle George. "Did they ever build castles that weren't on the top of hills?" Anne wanted to know. "Yes," replied Uncle George, "I can think of some castles that were built to defend the mouths of rivers. They are on the flat ground, near the river, and the ground often rises up behind them."

Uncle George went on to explain that castles like this one were built from about eight hundred years ago, up to about four hundred years ago. "It's often quite hard to say how old a castle is," he went on, "because castles were often altered, or added to, as the centuries went by. The oldest parts of a castle can easily be four hundred years older than the newest parts."

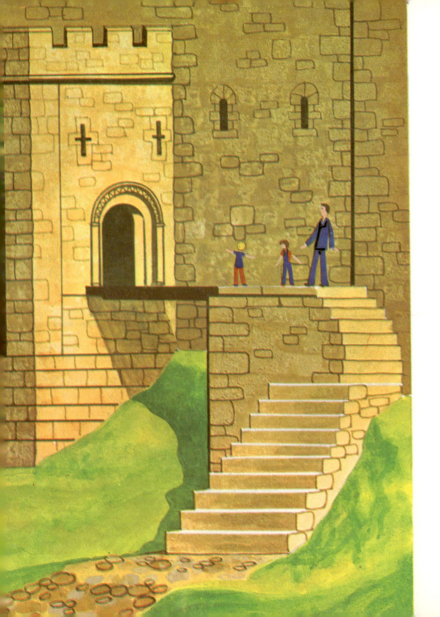

They climbed some stone steps that led to the "front door" of the keep. At the top of them was another drawbridge, though this time there was no moat. However, the children could see that, when the bridge was up, it would be very hard to get to the 'front door.' Uncle George explained that many castles had ordinary, big doors at this point, and that sometimes the drawbridge had been replaced by a solid stone bridge.

"This door is often the only way into the keep," said Uncle George, "so that if attackers had got this far, they could still only get into the keep two or three at a time, and quite a small number of determined men could hold this door against an army. By now you will have realised that everything about a castle was carefully designed to give the advantage to the people who were inside the castle. Everything was worked out to make things as hard as possible for attackers trying to get in."

The keep was really a tower, with very thick walls, and spiral stairways led to the upper and lower floors. "Here's another trick of the castle builders," said Uncle George, pointing to a spiral stairway. "Notice that it turns to the right as you go up. Nearly all the stairs in castles are like this. It means that enemies who were trying to fight their way up the stairs would find it more difficult to swing their swords properly, because of the pillar which runs up the middle. The defenders, up above them, had the advantage of space on their right hand, as well as height."

"That's jolly clever," said Tony, who was waving his arms around a few steps up. Meanwhile Anne had gone down towards the basement. "It would work the other way for enemies trying to come down here," she said, "they'd be better off than the defenders." "That's right," said Uncle George, grinning, "but there is only the basement down there. Let's go and look at it."

So they went down stairs to the basement. It was one big room, roughly round, and built of a number of archways, running round in a circle. "See how all these arches have one side at the centre of the room," said Uncle George, "That makes a big fat column in the middle, which carries all the weight of the floors above. Not all castles are like this. Many don't have a basement, or there are a few cells joined by tunnels." "Is this where they kept their prisoners?" asked Anne. "Perhaps," replied Uncle George, "they might be chained to those iron rings in the wall, and there would probably be straw on the floor for them to sleep on."

The basement wasn't a very nice place. It was cold, and gloomy, and the children were quite pleased when Uncle George led the way back up the stairs to the upper floors of the keep.

On the way up they found slit windows, which were much wider inside than out, and gave a good view of the surrounding country.

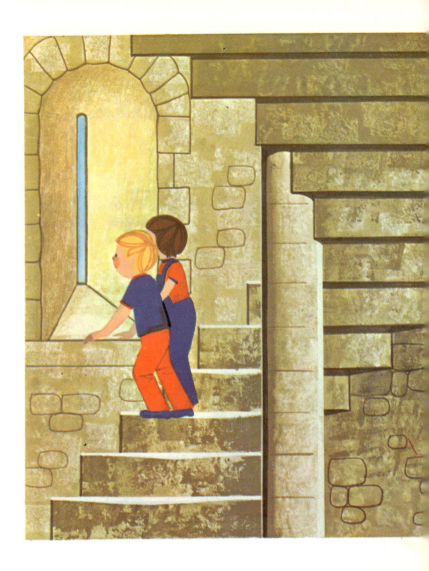

On the entrance floor, the keep was divided into a number of rooms. One was a kitchen, another might have been a guest room, another, a store room. Then they went up to the floor above, where there was one big room, with a wooden floor, and windows that were bigger than the others they had seen in the castle.

"This would be where the lord of the castle and his family lived," Uncle George explained. "This was usually called the solar, and was by far the most comfortable place in the whole castle. You can imagine the noble lord, sat writing, while his wife got on with the many tasks that fell to her in the running of this big place."

"Where are the bedrooms?" Anne wanted to know. "There aren't any that are just bedrooms and nothing else." Uncle George replied. "The lord and his family would have slept in the solar, and the servants and soldiers mostly slept where they worked. The grooms would have slept in the stables, the cooks in the kitchen, and the soldiers in the guard room. There are castles with bedrooms, or bed chambers as they are called, but they are the later castles, not the older ones."

By now Tony had found the stairs that led up to the roof of the keep, and from there the view was wonderful. Looking out over the battlements, they really could see for miles.

"In olden times," said Uncle George, "there would be soldiers on duty up here keeping watch day and night. You can see for your-selves that in the daytime an enemy could be spotted when he was miles away."

Uncle George and the children sat down in the sunshine and fresh air on the top of the keep. From there, Tony pointed out the tiny moving shape of a man on a bike, who must have been two miles away. "But it would not be so easy at night," he said "I should think that an enemy might sneak up in the dark." "Very few nights are completely dark," replied Uncle George, "From above, it is surprising how much movement you can pick out, even at night."

"But surely life in the castle wasn't all battles," said Anne, "Didn't they have feasts?" "Yes," smiled Uncle George. "Sometimes the whole of the castle household sat down to enjoy a great feast. In this castle, as in many others, the banquetting hall once stood in the outer bailey, though some castles had a great hall in the keep.

"An important part of life in the days of castles was called heraldry," Uncle George went on, "Every knight had his crest, and his coat of arms. One knight looked very much like another in armour, and so they used to carry crests on their helmets. The coat of arms was on the shield, or on a coat which was worn over the armour."

"Heraldry started as a very simple thing," Uncle George went on, "but it ended up by being very complicated. An expert could not only tell who a knight was by looking at his coat of arms, but also quite a lot about his family. And, of course, castles also started by being simple, and became more complex as time went on."

"The earliest castles of all, in this part of the world, were built more than a thousand years ago, and many of them were simply hill-tops, fortified with a wooden stockade. Then moats were added, and outer stockades, until they had something that was very like this castle. The next step, of course, was to build much more strongly in stone."

"Are there castles in other lands?" asked Anne, as Uncle George paused. "Oh yes," he replied, "especially in Europe. Some are very like this castle, though some look rather different, because they are built with different materials—the materials that they could get easily. Many castles in France have rooves over the battlements."

"Some castles in Germany, near the river Rhine, and others in Switzerland and central Europe are like this. Many of them hang on the edge of cliffs, high up on a mountain side, and they can only be approached at all from one direction. Then there are the castles built on flat ground, to defend river mouths. They are different."

catapult

battering ram

scaling ladder

siege tower

"How did they attack castles in those days?" asked Tony. "They didn't have guns, did they?" "There were no guns in the great days of castles," agreed Uncle George, "but they had what they called 'engines of war'. Some of these were huge catapults, that could hurl stone shot, or fire-balls."

"Then they had battering rams, for smashing doors. But perhaps the strongest weapon an enemy could use against a castle was a seige. In a seige, the enemy would surround a castle, and make sure that no food got in. Then they would use seige towers to attack the tops of the walls."

"I said just now that there were no guns in the great days of castles," said Uncle George as they walked down the stairs on their way out of the keep. "As a matter of fact, it was the coming of guns that ended the great days of castles."

Uncle George led the children around the side of the keep to a spot within the walls where an ancient cannon stood on a stone platform. It was green with age, and did not look very terrible. "Cannons like this could shoot a heavy ball of stone or iron with far greater force than any catapult," he explained, "so that the thickest wooden doors could be smashed, and even thick stone walls would be cracked by gunfire."

"Couldn't they build stronger walls?" asked Anne. "Yes," replied Uncle George, and this is what they did at first. But then the gunsmiths built bigger and better guns, until no stone wall could withstand their power, and the great days of the castles were numbered."